PRINCEWILL LAGANG

Intimacy Unveiled: Secrets to a Fulfilling Relationship

First published by PRINCEWILL LAGANG 2023

Copyright © 2023 by Princewill Lagang

All rights reserved. No part of this publication may be reproduced, stored or transmitted in any form or by any means, electronic, mechanical, photocopying, recording, scanning, or otherwise without written permission from the publisher. It is illegal to copy this book, post it to a website, or distribute it by any other means without permission.

Princewill Lagang asserts the moral right to be identified as the author of this work.

First edition

This book was professionally typeset on Reedsy.
Find out more at reedsy.com

Contents

1. Introduction to Intimacy Unveiled ... 1
2. The Layers of Emotional Intimacy ... 4
3. Physical Intimacy: Beyond the Surface ... 7
4. Communication as the Key to Intimacy ... 10
5. Vulnerability and Trust ... 13
6. Rediscovering Passion and Desire ... 16
7. Cultivating Spiritual Intimacy ... 19
8. Navigating Conflict with Intimacy ... 22
9. Intimacy Beyond the Bedroom ... 25
10. Self-Intimacy and Self-Care ... 28
11. Intimacy in a Digital Age ... 31
12. Sustaining Intimacy for a Lifetime ... 34

1

Introduction to Intimacy Unveiled

In the complex tapestry of human relationships, there exists a profound and deeply sought-after connection known as intimacy. It is a concept that transcends mere physical proximity or casual acquaintance, delving into the realms of emotional closeness, trust, vulnerability, and profound understanding. In this journey through the pages of "Intimacy Unveiled," we embark on a quest to uncover the secrets to cultivating a fulfilling and meaningful connection.

Defining Intimacy in the Context of Relationships

Before we begin our exploration, it is imperative to define intimacy as it pertains to relationships. Intimacy, in its most comprehensive sense, encompasses various dimensions that contribute to the depth of a connection between individuals. It is more than just a romantic notion; it extends to friendships, familial bonds, and even professional relationships.

1. Emotional Intimacy: At the core of intimacy lies emotional closeness. It involves the ability to share one's thoughts, feelings, and innermost desires with another person. Emotional intimacy fosters a sense of belonging and

allows individuals to be truly seen and understood by their partners.

2. Physical Intimacy: Physical closeness and affection play a significant role in relationships. It includes touch, hugs, kisses, and sexual intimacy. Physical intimacy is a means through which individuals express love, desire, and a sense of security.

3. Intellectual Intimacy: Beyond emotions and physicality, intellectual intimacy involves stimulating conversations, shared interests, and mutual respect for each other's thoughts and ideas. It enables partners to engage in meaningful discussions and grow together intellectually.

4. Spiritual Intimacy: For some, spiritual intimacy is a profound aspect of connection. It involves sharing one's spiritual beliefs, values, and a sense of purpose. This form of intimacy can be a powerful force in relationships, providing a sense of unity and purpose.

5. Trust and Vulnerability: Intimacy requires a foundation of trust and vulnerability. It necessitates the courage to let down walls and share one's true self, knowing that you will be accepted and supported by your partner.

Setting the Stage for Exploring the Secrets to a Fulfilling Connection

As we delve into the exploration of intimacy, it is essential to recognize that there are no one-size-fits-all solutions. Relationships are as unique as the individuals involved in them, and what fosters intimacy in one partnership may differ from another. However, there are universal principles, strategies, and practices that can help nurture and strengthen intimacy.

Throughout the chapters of "Intimacy Unveiled," we will embark on a comprehensive journey through these principles. We will uncover the intricacies of communication, trust-building, conflict resolution, and the role of empathy in fostering intimacy. We will also explore the impact of past experiences, societal influences, and personal growth on our ability to connect deeply with others.

In our quest to unveil the secrets to a fulfilling connection, we invite you to reflect on your own experiences and relationships. Consider what intimacy means to you and the ways in which you aspire to enhance the connections in your life. Whether you are seeking to enrich an existing relationship or embark on a new one, the insights within these pages aim to guide you towards a more profound, authentic, and satisfying sense of intimacy.

As we turn the page to Chapter 2, we will begin our journey by examining the cornerstone of intimacy: effective communication. For it is through communication that we build bridges of understanding, paving the way for deeper and more meaningful connections.

2

The Layers of Emotional Intimacy

Understanding Emotional Intimacy and Its Role in Relationships

Emotional intimacy is the foundational layer upon which strong and lasting relationships are built. It's the ability to connect with another person on a deep emotional level, sharing your innermost thoughts, feelings, and vulnerabilities without fear of judgment. This chapter explores the significance of emotional intimacy and offers techniques to cultivate and strengthen it in your relationships.

The Role of Emotional Intimacy:

1. Fosters Trust: Emotional intimacy creates a safe space where trust can thrive. When you can openly share your feelings and thoughts, you build a foundation of trust with your partner. This trust forms the basis for a healthy and enduring connection.

2. Enhances Communication: Effective communication is impossible without emotional intimacy. It's the key to understanding each other's needs, desires, and concerns. When emotional barriers are lowered, conversations

become more meaningful and productive.

3. Strengthens Connection: Emotional intimacy deepens the bond between partners. It's what transforms a mere acquaintance into a confidant, a friend into a soulmate. This level of connection provides a sense of security and belonging in the relationship.

Techniques for Opening Up and Deepening Emotional Bonds:

1. Active Listening: To foster emotional intimacy, practice active listening. When your partner speaks, give them your full attention. Validate their feelings and show empathy by acknowledging their emotions, even if you don't agree with them.

2. Share Your Feelings: Take the initiative to share your own feelings and thoughts. Vulnerability is a cornerstone of emotional intimacy. Express your fears, hopes, and dreams honestly, allowing your partner to see the real you.

3. Practice Empathy: Try to understand your partner's perspective, even when it differs from your own. Empathy creates an atmosphere of acceptance and support, making it easier for both of you to open up emotionally.

4. Create a Safe Space: Ensure that your relationship is a judgment-free zone. Encourage your partner to express themselves without fear of criticism. Respect their boundaries and show appreciation for their honesty.

5. Quality Time Together: Spend quality time with your partner. Shared experiences and activities can help create emotional connections. Whether it's a date night or simply relaxing together, these moments strengthen the emotional bond.

6. Conflict Resolution: Conflict is a natural part of any relationship. Learn to resolve conflicts constructively by focusing on the issue at hand rather

than attacking each other personally. Addressing conflicts with empathy and respect can deepen emotional intimacy.

7. Support Each Other's Growth: Encourage personal growth and self-discovery in your partner. Emotional intimacy isn't about stifling individuality but supporting each other's journey towards becoming the best version of yourselves.

8. Seek Professional Help if Needed: If you find it challenging to open up emotionally or face persistent communication issues, don't hesitate to seek the assistance of a relationship counselor or therapist. They can provide valuable guidance in navigating these challenges.

Emotional intimacy is an ongoing process that requires effort and commitment from both partners. As you peel back the layers of emotional vulnerability, you'll discover a deeper connection and a more fulfilling relationship. In Chapter 3, we'll explore the intricacies of physical intimacy and how it complements emotional closeness in building a well-rounded connection.

3

Physical Intimacy: Beyond the Surface

Physical intimacy is a vital component of human relationships, encompassing a wide range of expressions that go beyond mere touch. In this chapter, we delve into the various facets of physical intimacy and provide strategies for nurturing a satisfying and fulfilling physical connection in your relationship.

Exploring the Different Facets of Physical Intimacy:

1. Touch and Affection: Physical intimacy often begins with simple gestures of touch and affection. Holding hands, hugging, cuddling, and kissing are all expressions of love and closeness. Regular physical touch helps maintain a strong bond between partners.

2. Sexual Intimacy: Sexual intimacy is a deeply personal and shared experience between partners. It involves not only the physical act but also emotional connection and communication. Open and honest dialogue about desires, boundaries, and preferences is crucial in this aspect of intimacy.

3. Non-Sexual Physical Connection: Physical intimacy extends beyond the

bedroom. Simple acts like a comforting hug after a tough day, a massage, or even dancing together can enhance the physical connection between partners.

4. Intimacy of Presence: Sometimes, physical intimacy is as simple as being present for your partner. Sitting in silence, holding hands, or sharing a quiet moment together can be profoundly intimate.

Strategies for Maintaining a Satisfying and Fulfilling Physical Connection:

1. Effective Communication: Discuss your physical needs and desires openly with your partner. Be receptive to their needs as well. Establishing clear communication about boundaries, fantasies, and expectations is vital.

2. Quality Time Together: Dedicate time to nurture physical intimacy. Schedule regular date nights or weekend getaways to rekindle the spark and focus on each other without distractions.

3. Variety and Spontaneity: Keep things exciting by introducing variety into your physical relationship. Try new experiences, explore fantasies together, and be open to spontaneity.

4. Emotional Connection: Remember that emotional intimacy and physical intimacy are intertwined. Strengthening your emotional bond can enhance physical closeness and vice versa. Engage in activities that promote emotional connection, such as deep conversations and shared experiences.

5. Prioritize Self-Care: Taking care of your physical and emotional well-being is essential for maintaining a fulfilling physical connection. Exercise, eat healthily, and manage stress to ensure you have the energy and mindset for intimacy.

6. Educate Yourself: Learn about each other's bodies and what brings pleasure and satisfaction. Knowledge and understanding can lead to a more enjoyable

physical connection.

7. Practice Consent and Respect: Always prioritize consent and respect in your physical interactions. Both partners should feel safe and comfortable at all times. If either partner expresses discomfort, pause and communicate openly.

8. Seek Professional Help When Needed: If you encounter challenges in your physical intimacy, such as difficulties with desire, performance, or intimacy-related conflicts, consider consulting a therapist or sex therapist who specializes in relationship and sexual issues.

Physical intimacy can be a source of immense pleasure, connection, and fulfillment in a relationship. By exploring its diverse facets and nurturing it with care, you can cultivate a physical connection that enriches your partnership and strengthens the overall bond between you and your partner. In Chapter 4, we will delve into intellectual intimacy and the role of shared interests and meaningful conversations in deepening your connection.

4

Communication as the Key to Intimacy

Effective communication is the cornerstone of any intimate relationship. It's the means by which partners connect, understand, and support each other. In this chapter, we will explore how communication nurtures intimacy and provide techniques for active listening, empathy, and fostering meaningful conversations.

How Effective Communication Nurtures Intimacy:

1. Creates Understanding: Communication allows partners to share their thoughts, feelings, and experiences. Through open and honest dialogue, you can gain a deeper understanding of each other's perspectives and emotions, fostering a sense of connection.

2. Builds Trust: Trust is built through transparent and consistent communication. When you communicate openly, it signals to your partner that you are trustworthy and reliable, strengthening the foundation of your relationship.

3. Resolves Conflict: Conflicts are inevitable in any relationship. Effective communication helps in addressing and resolving these conflicts construc-

tively. It allows you to express your concerns, listen to your partner's viewpoint, and work together to find solutions.

4. Enhances Emotional Intimacy: Sharing your innermost thoughts and feelings through communication deepens emotional intimacy. It's a way to be vulnerable with your partner, allowing them to see your true self.

5. Promotes Empathy: Communication enables partners to understand each other's emotions and needs. This understanding fosters empathy, creating a supportive and compassionate environment.

Techniques for Active Listening, Empathy, and Fostering Meaningful Conversations:

1. Active Listening:
   - Give your full attention when your partner is speaking.
   - Avoid interrupting or formulating a response while they talk.
   - Use verbal and non-verbal cues (nodding, eye contact) to show that you're engaged in the conversation.
   - Reflect back what you've heard to ensure you've understood correctly.

2. Empathy:
   - Put yourself in your partner's shoes to understand their perspective.
   - Use phrases like "I can imagine how you must feel" to convey empathy.
   - Ask open-ended questions to encourage your partner to share their thoughts and emotions.

3. Fostering Meaningful Conversations:
   - Create a safe and non-judgmental space for discussions.
   - Initiate conversations about important topics, including dreams, goals, and fears.
   - Share your own thoughts and feelings openly to set an example.
   - Be patient and allow your partner time to express themselves.

4. Effective Expression:
   - Use "I" statements to express your feelings and needs without blaming or accusing.
   - Be specific and clear in your communication to avoid misunderstandings.
   - Choose the right moment for important conversations, ensuring both you and your partner are in a receptive state of mind.

5. Conflict Resolution:
   - When conflicts arise, practice active listening and empathy.
   - Avoid defensive or accusatory language.
   - Seek common ground and work together to find solutions.
   - If emotions escalate, take a break and return to the conversation later when both parties are calmer.

6. Practice Mindfulness: Being present in the moment during conversations can improve the quality of communication. Put away distractions and focus on the person you are speaking with.

7. Counseling or Therapy: If you encounter persistent communication challenges, consider seeking the assistance of a relationship counselor or therapist. They can provide guidance and strategies for improving communication.

Effective communication is an ongoing process that requires effort and practice. By honing your communication skills, you can create an environment where intimacy flourishes, and your connection with your partner deepens. In Chapter 5, we will explore intellectual intimacy, emphasizing the importance of shared interests and meaningful conversations in strengthening your bond.

5

Vulnerability and Trust

In the intricate dance of human relationships, vulnerability and trust are interwoven threads that form the tapestry of intimacy. This chapter delves into the profound connection between vulnerability and building trust, offering insights into creating a safe space for sharing thoughts, feelings, and fears within your relationship.

The Connection Between Vulnerability and Building Trust:

1. Vulnerability as a Catalyst: Vulnerability is the act of exposing your true self, warts and all, to your partner. It involves sharing your deepest thoughts, feelings, insecurities, and fears. Paradoxically, it is through vulnerability that trust is nurtured. When you allow yourself to be vulnerable, you signal to your partner that you trust them enough to share your inner world.

2. Building Emotional Bonds: Vulnerability creates an emotional bond that is difficult to replicate through any other means. When you reveal your authentic self and allow your partner to do the same, it forges a unique connection based on honesty and mutual understanding.

3. Fostering Empathy: Vulnerability opens the door to empathy. When you share your vulnerabilities, your partner is more likely to respond with compassion and support. This deepens the emotional connection and builds trust in your relationship.

4. Strengthening Resilience: Facing vulnerability together can strengthen your resilience as a couple. When you weather challenges and insecurities together, you build a sense of unity and trust that can withstand adversity.

Creating a Safe Space for Sharing Thoughts, Feelings, and Fears:

1. Open and Non-Judgmental Communication: Encourage open and non-judgmental communication in your relationship. Let your partner know that their thoughts and feelings are valued and respected, regardless of whether they align with your own.

2. Active Listening: When your partner shares their vulnerabilities, practice active listening. Give them your full attention, avoid interrupting, and respond with empathy and understanding. Avoid offering immediate solutions; sometimes, they just need someone to listen.

3. Mutual Sharing: Vulnerability is a two-way street. Be willing to share your own thoughts, feelings, and fears with your partner. This reciprocity fosters trust and demonstrates that you trust them enough to be vulnerable in return.

4. Patience and Support: When your partner opens up, respond with patience and support. Avoid criticism or judgment. Instead, offer reassurance and encouragement.

5. Boundaries and Consent: Respect your partner's boundaries. Not everyone is comfortable sharing everything all at once. Ensure that both of you are on the same page regarding what can be shared and when.

6. Forgiveness and Understanding: Understand that vulnerability may lead to uncomfortable truths or past mistakes. Be prepared to forgive and offer understanding when your partner shares difficult experiences.

7. Seek Professional Guidance: If there are significant barriers to vulnerability or trust within your relationship, consider seeking the assistance of a therapist or counselor. They can provide guidance on overcoming obstacles and creating a more open and trusting dynamic.

Vulnerability and trust are essential elements of intimacy that require time, patience, and effort to cultivate. By creating a safe space for open and honest communication, you can strengthen the bonds of trust in your relationship, allowing intimacy to flourish. In Chapter 6, we will explore the role of shared values and goals in deepening your connection, emphasizing the importance of aligning your life visions with your partner.

6

Rediscovering Passion and Desire

Passion and desire are like the flickering flames of a candle, enchanting in their early stages, but in long-term relationships, they can sometimes wane. In this chapter, we will explore the dynamics of passion and desire within committed partnerships and offer strategies for reigniting the spark through intentional efforts and exploration.

Understanding the Dynamics of Passion and Desire in Long-Term Relationships:

1. Evolution of Passion: In the initial stages of a relationship, passion often burns brightly, driven by novelty, physical attraction, and the thrill of discovery. However, as time goes on, this initial intensity may naturally ebb.

2. Challenges to Desire: Long-term relationships face various challenges that can dampen desire, including routine, stress, and familiarity. Responsibilities such as work, children, and household chores can take precedence over intimate connection.

3. Differentiation Between Passion and Love: It's important to recognize that while the intensity of passion may fluctuate, love can deepen over time. Long-lasting love often incorporates qualities such as companionship, trust, and emotional intimacy, which provide a sturdy foundation for passionate connection.

Reigniting the Spark Through Intentional Efforts and Exploration:

1. Prioritize Intimacy: Make intimacy a priority in your relationship. Set aside time for romantic and physical connection, even amidst busy schedules. Date nights, weekend getaways, and spontaneous gestures can rekindle passion.

2. Open Communication: Discuss your desires and fantasies with your partner openly and without judgment. Effective communication about your needs and boundaries is essential for reigniting passion.

3. Variety and Novelty: Inject novelty into your relationship. Explore new activities, hobbies, or experiences together. Novelty can rekindle excitement and desire.

4. Physical Connection: Physical intimacy is a significant aspect of passion. Experiment with different ways of physical connection, such as massages, shared baths, or trying new sexual experiences that both partners are comfortable with.

5. Maintain Individuality: While sharing a life together, it's crucial to maintain individuality. Pursue personal interests, hobbies, and goals. A sense of autonomy can make you more interesting and attractive to your partner.

6. Surprise and Spontaneity: Surprise your partner with unexpected acts of love and affection. Leave love notes, plan a surprise dinner, or simply express

your affection in unexpected ways.

7. Quality Time: Spend quality time together without distractions. This means putting away phones and focusing on each other. Quality time is a powerful way to reignite emotional and physical connection.

8. Explore Together: Explore new things as a couple. This can include trying new hobbies, traveling to new destinations, or learning something new together. These shared experiences can reignite passion and create lasting memories.

9. Seek Professional Help: If you're struggling to reignite passion and desire in your relationship, consider couples' therapy or counseling. A therapist can provide guidance and techniques tailored to your specific needs.

Rediscovering passion and desire in a long-term relationship is a journey that requires effort, creativity, and dedication from both partners. By intentionally nurturing your connection and exploring new aspects of your partnership, you can breathe new life into your relationship, deepening your bond and reigniting the flames of passion. In Chapter 7, we will explore the role of commitment and resilience in maintaining a fulfilling and lasting connection.

7

Cultivating Spiritual Intimacy

While intimacy often conjures images of emotional and physical connection, it also extends to the spiritual dimension of human relationships. In this chapter, we'll explore the profound role of spiritual intimacy, the sharing of values, beliefs, and practices, in deepening the connection between partners.

Exploring the Spiritual Dimension of Intimacy:

1. Defining Spiritual Intimacy: Spiritual intimacy transcends religious affiliations and encompasses the shared understanding of life's deeper meaning and purpose. It involves connecting on a spiritual level, regardless of one's specific belief system.

2. The Quest for Meaning: Humans often seek meaning in their lives, and exploring spirituality with a partner can provide a sense of purpose and direction. It involves asking profound questions about existence, ethics, and morality.

3. Connection to Something Greater: Spiritual intimacy often involves a

sense of connection to something greater than oneself, whether that's a higher power, nature, the universe, or the collective human experience.

Sharing Values, Beliefs, and Practices that Deepen the Connection:

1. Open Dialogue: Initiate open and respectful conversations about your spiritual beliefs, values, and experiences. Create a safe space for both partners to share their perspectives without judgment.

2. Shared Rituals and Practices: Engage in shared spiritual rituals or practices, if both partners are comfortable with this. It can be as simple as meditation, prayer, or attending spiritual gatherings together. These shared experiences can strengthen your spiritual bond.

3. Respect for Differences: Recognize that you and your partner may have different spiritual beliefs or paths. Respect these differences, and focus on the values and principles that unite you.

4. Exploring Together: Explore new spiritual ideas or philosophies together. Read books, attend workshops, or engage in discussions that broaden your understanding of spirituality as a couple.

5. Supporting Growth: Encourage each other's spiritual growth and self-discovery. Understand that spiritual journeys can evolve over time, and support your partner in their exploration.

6. Mindful Presence: Practice mindful presence in your relationship. Be fully present in the moment and appreciate the spiritual connection you share.

7. Acts of Service: Engage in acts of service together, such as volunteering or helping those in need. These actions can align with your shared spiritual values and deepen your sense of purpose as a couple.

8. Reflect on Shared Values: Periodically reflect on your shared values, beliefs, and the spiritual foundation of your relationship. This can reinforce your connection and remind you of your shared journey.

9. Counseling and Guidance: Seek guidance from spiritual leaders, counselors, or therapists who specialize in helping couples navigate spiritual issues. They can provide insights and tools to enhance your spiritual intimacy.

Cultivating spiritual intimacy can be a deeply enriching experience that adds a profound layer to your relationship. It allows you to explore life's most profound questions together and connect on a level that transcends the everyday. By nurturing this aspect of your partnership, you can strengthen your bond and create a lasting connection that reflects your shared spiritual journey. In Chapter 8, we'll explore the significance of trust and vulnerability in maintaining a fulfilling and meaningful relationship.

8

Navigating Conflict with Intimacy

Conflict is an inevitable part of any relationship, but it can be a potent force for growth and connection when handled with care. In this chapter, we'll explore how to utilize conflict as an opportunity for growth and connection, and we'll provide strategies for resolving conflicts while preserving intimacy.

Utilizing Conflict as an Opportunity for Growth and Connection:

1. Understanding Conflict's Role: Conflict arises from differences in perspectives, needs, and desires. Rather than viewing it as a threat, recognize that conflict is a natural part of human interaction and can lead to greater understanding when addressed constructively.

2. Opportunity for Learning: Conflict provides an opportunity to learn more about yourself and your partner. It can uncover hidden emotions, unmet needs, and areas for personal and relational growth.

3. Deepening Empathy: Successfully navigating conflict requires empathizing with your partner's perspective. When you do so, you foster empathy, which

can deepen emotional intimacy.

Strategies for Resolving Conflicts While Preserving Intimacy:

1. Effective Communication: Maintain open and respectful communication during conflicts. Avoid blaming, shaming, or name-calling. Use "I" statements to express your feelings and needs. Listen actively to your partner's perspective.

2. Choose the Right Time: Timing matters in conflict resolution. Address issues when both you and your partner are calm and able to engage in a productive conversation. Avoid discussing sensitive topics when emotions are running high.

3. Stay Focused on the Issue: During a conflict, stay focused on the specific issue at hand. Avoid bringing up past grievances, as this can derail the conversation and lead to more significant conflicts.

4. Seek Common Ground: Look for areas of agreement or compromise. Finding common ground can pave the way for resolution and demonstrate that you both value the relationship.

5. Empathize and Validate: Make an effort to understand your partner's perspective. Validate their feelings, even if you disagree with their viewpoint. Empathy can diffuse tension and foster connection.

6. Use Conflict Resolution Tools: Familiarize yourself with conflict resolution techniques, such as active listening, compromise, and problem-solving. These tools can help you address conflicts more effectively.

7. Take Breaks When Needed: If a conflict becomes too heated or unproductive, it's okay to take a break. Step away from the situation to cool down and collect your thoughts. Return to the conversation when you're both in a

better frame of mind.

8. Apologize and Forgive: Apologize when necessary and be willing to forgive. Holding onto grudges can erode trust and intimacy. Forgiveness is an essential part of moving forward.

9. Learn from Conflict: After a conflict is resolved, reflect on what you've learned. Use the experience to grow individually and as a couple. Consider what changes or compromises can prevent similar conflicts in the future.

10. Seek Professional Help: If you find that conflicts persist or become increasingly destructive, consider seeking the guidance of a relationship counselor or therapist. They can provide tools and strategies to navigate complex issues.

Navigating conflict with intimacy requires patience, empathy, and a commitment to preserving the bond between you and your partner. By approaching conflicts as opportunities for growth and using effective communication and conflict resolution strategies, you can transform moments of tension into opportunities for deeper connection. In the final chapter, we will wrap up our exploration of intimacy and provide insights into maintaining a fulfilling and lasting relationship.

9

Intimacy Beyond the Bedroom

Intimacy extends far beyond the confines of the bedroom. It's a multifaceted concept that can permeate every aspect of a relationship, enriching your connection with your partner. In this chapter, we'll explore the importance of expanding the boundaries of intimacy into everyday life and how you can connect deeply through shared experiences, hobbies, and quality time.

Expanding the Boundaries of Intimacy into Everyday Life:

1. A Holistic Approach: Intimacy isn't limited to physical closeness or emotional connection; it's a holistic concept that encompasses all aspects of a relationship. It's about being present with your partner, sharing moments, and nurturing your bond in various ways.

2. Connecting Beyond the Bedroom: Building intimacy beyond the bedroom involves weaving it into your daily life. It's about finding ways to maintain closeness, understanding, and shared experiences in your routines.

Connecting Through Shared Experiences, Hobbies, and Quality Time:

INTIMACY UNVEILED: SECRETS TO A FULFILLING RELATIONSHIP

1. Shared Interests: Explore shared interests and hobbies. Whether it's a passion for hiking, cooking, painting, or a love for a particular genre of movies, engaging in activities you both enjoy can create moments of connection.

2. Quality Time: Dedicate quality time to each other. This doesn't always have to be extravagant; even simple activities like cooking together, taking a leisurely walk, or cuddling on the couch can deepen your bond.

3. Unplug and Be Present: In our digital age, it's easy to get lost in screens and distractions. Make an effort to unplug and be present when you're spending time together. Genuine presence fosters deeper connection.

4. Create Rituals: Establish meaningful rituals or traditions that are unique to your relationship. These can be weekly date nights, special anniversary celebrations, or even daily moments like morning coffee together.

5. Adventure and Exploration: Embark on adventures or explore new places together. Traveling, even locally, can provide opportunities for shared experiences, learning, and creating lasting memories.

6. Open Communication: Continue to communicate openly and honestly in everyday life. Share your thoughts, feelings, and daily experiences with each other. Encourage your partner to do the same.

7. Express Appreciation: Don't forget to express appreciation regularly. Compliment each other, acknowledge each other's efforts, and say "I love you" often. These small gestures contribute to emotional intimacy.

8. Support Each Other: Be supportive of each other's goals and dreams. Encourage personal growth and celebrate each other's achievements, both big and small.

9. Mindful Eating: Share meals mindfully. Turn mealtime into an opportu-

nity to connect by engaging in meaningful conversation and savoring the experience together.

10. Laughter and Play: Don't underestimate the power of laughter and play. Engage in activities that make you both laugh and enjoy each other's company. Playfulness can reignite the spark in your relationship.

11. Random Acts of Kindness: Surprise each other with random acts of kindness. Small gestures like leaving sweet notes, making breakfast in bed, or planning a surprise outing can make a big difference.

Expanding intimacy beyond the bedroom is about embracing the totality of your relationship. It's about finding opportunities for connection, understanding, and shared experiences in everyday life. By nurturing intimacy in these diverse ways, you can create a relationship that is rich, fulfilling, and lasting. In our concluding chapter, we'll summarize key insights and provide a roadmap for maintaining a fulfilling and meaningful partnership.

10

Self-Intimacy and Self-Care

The foundation of any intimate relationship is the individual self. In this final chapter, we'll explore the critical concepts of self-intimacy and self-care, recognizing their importance in personal growth and how they contribute to deeper intimacy within your relationship.

Recognizing the Importance of Self-Awareness and Self-Love:

1. Self-Intimacy Defined: Self-intimacy is the process of getting to know oneself deeply and authentically. It involves understanding your emotions, beliefs, values, desires, and vulnerabilities. It's about creating a loving and compassionate relationship with yourself.

2. Self-Love: Self-love is the foundation of self-intimacy. It's the practice of treating yourself with kindness, respect, and care. It involves accepting your imperfections, embracing your uniqueness, and nurturing a positive self-image.

How Personal Growth and Self-Care Contribute to Relationship Intimacy:

SELF-INTIMACY AND SELF-CARE

1. Personal Growth: Personal growth is an ongoing journey of self-improvement and self-discovery. When individuals commit to their personal growth, they bring greater self-awareness, emotional intelligence, and resilience to their relationships.

- Emotional Intelligence: Growing emotionally allows you to navigate conflicts, communicate effectively, and empathize with your partner's feelings.

- Self-Awareness: Self-aware individuals can recognize and communicate their needs, boundaries, and desires, creating healthier relationships.

- Resilience: Personal growth builds resilience, which helps couples navigate challenges and bounce back from setbacks.

2. Self-Care: Self-care involves nurturing your physical, emotional, and mental well-being. When you prioritize self-care, you become better equipped to show up as your best self in your relationship.

- Physical Health: Maintaining good physical health through exercise, nutrition, and rest enhances your energy and vitality, allowing you to engage fully with your partner.

- Emotional Well-Being: Self-care practices like meditation, journaling, or therapy can help you manage stress, regulate emotions, and maintain emotional balance within your relationship.

- Mental Clarity: Taking time for mental self-care, such as practicing mindfulness or engaging in hobbies you enjoy, can clear your mind and allow you to be present with your partner.

The Connection Between Self-Intimacy, Self-Care, and Relationship Intimacy:

INTIMACY UNVEILED: SECRETS TO A FULFILLING RELATIONSHIP

1. Self-Intimacy as a Prerequisite: Before you can fully open up to another person, you must first establish a deep connection with yourself. Self-intimacy enables you to be vulnerable and authentic in your relationship.

2. Balancing Self-Care and Care for Others: Self-care ensures that you have the emotional and physical resources to care for your partner effectively. It prevents burnout and fosters resilience, enabling you to support each other during challenging times.

3. Enhancing Emotional Availability: When you practice self-care and self-intimacy, you become more emotionally available to your partner. You can share your feelings and vulnerabilities, allowing for a deeper emotional connection.

4. Maintaining Boundaries: Self-intimacy and self-care help you establish and maintain healthy boundaries within your relationship. This ensures that your needs are met while respecting your partner's boundaries as well.

5. Modeling Healthy Behavior: By prioritizing self-intimacy and self-care, you set an example for your partner to do the same. This creates a culture of self-awareness, growth, and well-being within your relationship.

In conclusion, self-intimacy and self-care are essential components of a healthy and fulfilling relationship. As you embark on your journey to deepen intimacy with your partner, don't forget to nurture your own growth, self-awareness, and well-being. By practicing self-love and personal development, you not only enhance your own life but also contribute to a more profound and lasting intimacy with your partner.

11

Intimacy in a Digital Age

In an increasingly technology-driven world, the landscape of intimacy is evolving. This chapter explores the challenges and opportunities of intimacy in the digital age, emphasizing the importance of balancing digital interactions with face-to-face connections.

Navigating the Challenges and Opportunities of Intimacy in a Technology-Driven World:

1. The Digital Shift: The advent of technology, especially smartphones and social media, has transformed the way we communicate and connect. While these tools offer new avenues for intimacy, they also bring challenges.

2. Opportunities for Connection: Technology can facilitate connection over long distances. It allows us to stay in touch with loved ones, share moments through photos and videos, and even engage in virtual dates or intimate conversations.

3. Challenges to Intimacy: Technology can also present challenges to intimacy. Overreliance on digital communication can lead to a lack of face-

to-face interaction, misunderstandings due to text-based communication, and distractions that hinder quality time with our partners.

Balancing Digital Interactions with Face-to-Face Connections:

1. Mindful Digital Usage: Practice mindful digital usage. Be aware of the time you spend on screens and how it affects your relationship. Set boundaries for screen time, especially during quality moments with your partner.

2. Prioritize Face-to-Face Interaction: While digital communication is valuable, prioritize face-to-face interaction. Spending time together without screens can strengthen your emotional connection and intimacy.

3. Quality over Quantity: Focus on the quality of your interactions, whether digital or in person. Meaningful conversations and genuine presence matter more than the frequency of communication.

4. Technology-Assisted Connection: Use technology as a tool to enhance your connection rather than replace it. Video calls, voice messages, and shared playlists can be ways to feel closer to your partner, especially when distance separates you.

5. Digital Detox: Periodically take a digital detox. Disconnect from screens and immerse yourself in real-life experiences with your partner. It's a great way to recharge and reconnect.

6. Use Technology to Plan Real-Life Activities: Use digital tools to plan real-life activities and experiences with your partner. Whether it's organizing a surprise date night or researching a new hobby to explore together, technology can facilitate in-person connections.

7. Practice Active Listening: When communicating digitally, practice active listening. Ensure you understand your partner's messages and feelings

accurately to avoid misunderstandings.

8. Digital Boundaries: Discuss digital boundaries with your partner. Be transparent about your comfort levels with sharing aspects of your relationship online and respecting each other's privacy.

9. Be Present: Whether you're communicating digitally or face-to-face, practice being present with your partner. Show genuine interest, empathy, and attention during your interactions.

10. Seek Balance: Balance is key. Strive to create a harmonious blend of digital and face-to-face interactions that support your relationship's unique dynamics.

Intimacy in a digital age presents both challenges and opportunities. By navigating this landscape mindfully, setting boundaries, and prioritizing face-to-face connections, you can harness the benefits of technology while preserving and deepening the intimacy in your relationship. In the final chapter, we will summarize key takeaways and offer concluding thoughts on nurturing lasting and meaningful intimacy.

12

Sustaining Intimacy for a Lifetime

Maintaining intimacy throughout a lifetime is a journey filled with challenges and rewards. In this final chapter, we'll reflect on the path you've taken and explore strategies for sustaining and nurturing intimacy as your relationship evolves.

Reflecting on the Journey of Maintaining Intimacy Over Time:

1. The Evolution of Intimacy: Recognize that intimacy evolves as your relationship matures. What might have ignited passion in the early days may give way to deeper emotional and spiritual connections as time goes on.

2. Challenges and Triumphs: Reflect on the challenges you've faced together and the triumphs you've celebrated. These experiences have shaped your connection and resilience as a couple.

3. Growth and Change: Understand that both you and your partner will change and grow over time. Embrace this growth as an opportunity to rediscover each other and your evolving connection.

SUSTAINING INTIMACY FOR A LIFETIME

Strategies for Ongoing Growth, Connection, and Nurturing Intimacy Throughout Life:

1. Continual Communication: Never stop communicating. Keep the channels of communication open, addressing evolving needs, desires, and goals as they arise.

2. Adaptability: Be adaptable to change. Life will present unexpected challenges and opportunities. Embrace change together, knowing that you can navigate it as a team.

3. Shared Goals: Continue to set and work toward shared goals. Whether they're related to your relationship, family, or personal growth, having common aspirations strengthens your bond.

4. Quality Time: Dedicate quality time to each other. Prioritize date nights, adventures, and moments of togetherness that nurture your emotional and physical connection.

5. Nurturing Individuality: Support each other's individual growth and passions. Encourage your partner to pursue their dreams and hobbies, and do the same for yourself. A sense of personal fulfillment enriches your partnership.

6. Regular Intimacy Check-Ins: Schedule regular "intimacy check-ins" where you discuss the state of your relationship, your needs, and your desires. This practice helps prevent issues from festering and promotes open communication.

7. Gratitude and Appreciation: Continue to express gratitude and appreciation for each other. Regularly acknowledge your partner's contributions to your life and relationship.

8. Renewing Romance: Rediscover the romance in your relationship. Surprise each other with gestures of love, plan special outings, and celebrate anniversaries and milestones.

9. Embrace Vulnerability: Embrace vulnerability as an ongoing practice. Share your thoughts, feelings, and fears with each other, fostering deeper emotional intimacy.

10. Seek Professional Help When Needed: If you encounter significant challenges or feel disconnected, don't hesitate to seek the guidance of a relationship counselor or therapist. They can provide valuable tools and insights.

11. Celebrate Each Other's Growth: Celebrate the growth and achievements of both partners. Acknowledge the ways in which you've each evolved and how your relationship has flourished as a result.

12. Keep the Spark Alive: Never lose sight of the spark that ignited your connection. Continue to explore and experiment with all facets of intimacy, from emotional to physical to spiritual.

Sustaining intimacy for a lifetime is a testament to your commitment and dedication as a couple. It's a journey of continual growth, connection, and adaptation to the ever-changing landscape of your relationship. By embracing change, nurturing your connection, and continually exploring the depths of intimacy, you can create a lasting and meaningful partnership that stands the test of time.

Conclusion: Intimacy Unveiled - Secrets to a Fulfilling Relationship

In the pages of "Intimacy Unveiled," we have embarked on a journey through the intricate tapestry of human connection, exploring the secrets to nurturing a fulfilling and lasting relationship. This voyage has taken us through the depths of emotional intimacy, the nuances of physical connection, the power of vulnerability and trust, and the significance of shared values and spirituality.

We've uncovered the art of communication as the key to intimacy, the rekindling of passion and desire, and the delicate navigation of conflicts as opportunities for growth and connection. We've ventured into the realms of self-intimacy and self-care, understanding that personal growth is the cornerstone of a thriving partnership.

In the digital age, we've learned to balance the opportunities and challenges technology brings to intimacy, ensuring that the screens that connect us never overshadow the warmth of face-to-face connection. Finally, we've contemplated the art of sustaining intimacy for a lifetime, knowing that this journey is a continuous evolution of growth, change, and renewal.

Through this exploration, we've uncovered the truth that intimacy isn't a fixed destination but a dynamic and ever-evolving process. It thrives when nurtured with intention, care, and a deep commitment to understanding and cherishing both oneself and one's partner.

As we conclude this journey, remember that the secrets to a fulfilling relationship lie not in a single formula or quick fix but in the ongoing practice of love, empathy, vulnerability, and respect. Embrace the ever-unfolding path of intimacy, recognizing that it is a journey well worth taking—a journey that leads to a lifetime of shared joys, growth, and the deep fulfillment of a love that stands the test of time.

www.ingramcontent.com/pod-product-compliance
Lightning Source LLC
LaVergne TN
LVHW021055100526
838202LV00083B/5996